MW00583206

THE DUCK AND THE BUTTERFLY:

Coaching Questions for Leaders at Work

ISBN   978-0-9959958-3-3   paperback

       978-0-9959958-2-6   ebook

TRIFOLD

THE DUCK AND THE BUTTERFLY

COACHING QUESTIONS FOR LEADERS AT WORK

NATALIE MICHAEL

DEDICATION

This book is dedicated to Chris and JaSi,
three (not two) curious souls.

INTRODUCTION
Ask Better Questions, Get Better Insights

A good question has the potential to transform reality. It can turn a conversation into a life-changing moment. It can wake up a team and inspire a revolution. And it can pivot a business into high growth. But how the heck do you come up with insightful questions when you need them? It's not so easy. *Until now.*

Whether you want to self-reflect, lead a team meeting, wow your colleagues in a strategy session, or coach a high-potential leader, there is a question in this book for you. After a decade of executive coaching, I have handcrafted, teased out, and tested the most powerful coaching questions so that you don't have to do it. What took me years to develop, you can apply in five minutes.

The concept behind this book is simple:

- Pick your topic

- Review the questions

- Select one or two questions that fit your situation

- Ask away

- And voilà! Your self-reflection and conversations will be qualitatively different than before

As you review and select your questions, keep in mind that there are years of research and experience underpinning these questions and the way they are organized. To create the questions, I tapped into research, workshops, and books on executive development, coaching, leadership, and business. My approach was to learn the best-practice research, distill the key points, and then flip the core ideas into questions, giving you plenty of angles for exploring a topic. Then, my coaching practice became my "lab"—the place where I tested and refined the material you see here.

Equally relevant, I tested many of the questions on myself, seeing firsthand how powerful they could be. To be candid, when I was writing this book, I was entering a new phase of my life. Although I had achieved many outward signs of success, at forty-four I felt that something was missing and

I needed to change my life setup. A still small voice was speaking to me, and it was saying that the best years of my life lay before me, yet to make a shift toward something more significant, I needed to discover my mission and purpose, and reorient my life toward new values that were more holistic and more expansive than achievement goals and cash. Many of the questions in this book helped me to pinpoint what brings meaning to my life and relationships, and they helped me to sharpen my business focus in valuable ways. Some of the personal questions that helped me the most were:

- *What is Spirit calling you to do?*

- *What goal feels like a mission or calling?*

- *What career choices align with who you want to be as a parent?*

- *What would an ideal year look like for you?*

And in the business realm:

- *If you could put 5 percent of your time toward something deeply meaningful to you, what would it be?*

- *If you were to create a new business, how could you best serve others?*

- *What is your true differentiation in the marketplace?*

Thanks to the questions in this book, I formulated an expansive vision for my next life chapter. I redefined my work in meaningful ways, clarified what life fulfillment means to me, and recognized the importance of having a spiritual dimension in my life. Now, I am learning to say "yes" to my heart, and to say "no" more often. Counterintuitively, more (not less) opportunity seems to be coming my way.

Beyond this, I learned firsthand that a good question is one that opens the mind, invites truth, and evokes new possibilities. It's a catalyst for self-reflection and meaningful dialogue, and it has the power to make a difference in someone's life, sparking positive change.

To put it simply, I learned this book is much more than a pile of questions. More broadly, it's a toolkit for changing lives—including mine and, hopefully, yours.

How to Use This Book

There are three sections in this book centered on common issues that leaders face when coaching others. Not surprisingly, each section includes lots of questions. Although the book is written specifically for leaders, it is also relevant for board members, executive coaches, facilitators, volunteers, and individuals keen to self-reflect.

The three sections are:

1. **Leading Your Life** – Section 1 is all about finding a meaningful career path, living on purpose, uncovering values, and having energy. It's designed to give you and the people you coach a life tune-up and sharper focus on what really matters.

2. **Leading Others** – Section 2 will help you be a better leader. You will find questions that will better prepare you to coach high-potential talent on common issues, such as refining one's leadership style, being more influential, and delegating. You will also find questions designed to improve team dynamics and team work.

3. **Leading Organizations** – Section 3 will help you lead strategy and operations, boost innovation, and improve culture. The questions focus on the organization as a whole and will give you fresh inquiries for team and strategy sessions.

As you read this book, you will notice there is some overlap across the sections, as they are interdependent. Every professional needs to develop the skills necessary to lead their life, lead others, and lead organizations, and it's not unusual to bring several of these skills to bear in any given conversation. Familiarize yourself with each section to find how all the pieces fit together for your specific situation.

As a bonus, there is a final section with zinger questions about macrolevel issues prevalent in the world. Have fun with these! My hope is that you will find them profound. But I will be satisfied if, at the very least, you use them at your next dinner party to spark some meaningful (and hopefully entertaining) dialogue.

Here are some teasers from the bonus section:

- If you could write a message that would get through to all of humanity, what would your message be?

- What would you like to be different in the world for the next generation?

- How is technology changing what it feels like to be human?

The Duck and the Butterfly

Throughout the book, you will find a duck icon and a butterfly icon, indicating there are tips for effective listening and delivering your questions in a positive way. If you follow these tips, you will create meaningful dialogue, touch people deeply, and avoid mundane exchanges.

THE DUCK

Throughout the book, the duck icon symbolizes a listening tip. You might ask, why a duck?

It's a reminder: When you ask a great question,
you need to *shut the duck up!*

L-I-S-T-E-N to the answer.
(Easier said than done for most people.)

This requires a strong intention—one to listen without interrupting, jumping in with advice, or being distracted by what's next on your calendar.

If you want to be effective with your questions, the time to start listening is now. Follow the listening tips throughout the book to understand better what great listening looks, feels, and sounds like.

THE BUTTERFLY

You will also find a butterfly icon, a reminder that a question has transformational potential when it is delivered in such a way that it opens people up rather than shutting them down.

 If you ask a question with open and thoughtful energy, the question can create the space for a person or team to evolve and grow. Contrast this with a question that hits people like a sledge-hammer—one that seems more like a beating than an inquiry.

How you deliver the question counts.

When you put the butterfly tips into practice, you will not only ask a question; you will also create a positive experience.

"JUST LIVING"

Just living is not enough,

Said the butterfly.

One must have sunshine, freedom,

And a little flower.

—*Hans Christian Andersen*

Seven Ways to Apply the Questions

To help you, here are seven suggestions for applying these questions to your personal life and to different work settings.

1. **As a Journaling Tool** – If you want to be more purposeful about your life and career and you enjoy self-reflection, you can use these questions as a journaling tool. Put this book by your bedside, flip open to a page, and see what questions pop out at you. This will give your journaling some rigor with an intuitive twist.

2. **Discussion Starters** – When coaching others, pick a question to kick off your coaching sessions and/or jot a few questions down before heading into a coaching session so that you don't get stuck without anything meaningful to ask. Alternatively, pick a "question for the week" that you use for all your coaching sessions to set the tone and enrich discussions.

3. **Coaching and Team Inquiries** – After a workshop or coaching session, give team members a question to reflect on as a homework assignment to deepen insight and learning.

4. **Dinner Games** – If you have a dinner party with your friends or teammates, these questions can make the evening fun. Consider writing questions on cards and using them as conversation starters between dinner courses, or give a question to each guest and request that throughout the meal, each guest make a toast and answer his or her respective questions.

5. **Team Agendas** – Consider adding a few questions to your team agendas, or get your team to go through the book together and pick a few questions they want to explore.

6. **Preparation for Executive Meetings** – Let's face it, you can never be too prepared for executive meetings, especially if you want to elevate discussions and stand out from your peers. Come prepared with a few questions to ask your peers or team members so that your discussions are strategic, not mundane.

7. **Exploring Strategic Issues** – For strategic planning sessions, it is beneficial to pick four questions that explore a topic from different angles. Write them on flip charts, and have participants break out into small groups to explore each question and then report their answers to the broader group.

Thank You

A heartfelt thank-you for picking up this book and being inspired to ask better questions. Personally, I love that "coaching moment" when I ask a question and someone gasps at the sheer enormity of its potential, saying, "Ohh, now *that's* a really powerful question." I can't wait for this to happen to you!

Menu of Coaching Topics

Section 1

LEADING YOUR LIFE

> There is no passion to be found playing
> small—in settling for a life that is less
> than the one you are capable of living.
> —*Nelson Mandela*

Many people wake up tired in the morning not because they didn't sleep enough, but because they are not energized by their day ahead. Don't go through your life groggy, or let the people around you do the same. The questions in this section help you clarify what success means to you, helping you pinpoint what is truly significant and meaningful for your life. On this same track, the questions will help you to coach others on these topics and more.

If you are like most of my clients, answering these questions will likely reveal the joy of the simple things in life: creating something with like-minded people, having a good night's sleep, reading an inspiring book, or helping a family member in need. But the questions may also reveal answers to bigger, more complex questions: How will the world be different as a result of your contribution, long after you are gone? And what trade-offs or discomforts are you willing to endure in pursuit of your values and dreams? This last question is one that I consider central to a life well lived. It's freeing to acknowledge that even the best laid plans won't be accompanied by unicorns and sunshine every day, but the turmoil is worth it when your life aligns around your deepest passions and core values.

I can say from experience that if you ask yourself or others some of the questions in this section, you will find opportunities to discover greater meaning, cohesion, and significance. You will likely shake things up in your life, as you tap into your mind and heart.

1. Leading Your Life

DUCK

A coaching conversation is different from a superficial conversation. It's a unique opportunity to really listen to another person and pay attention to where they are in the journey of life.

BUTTERFLY

When you ask questions, watch your tone so it doesn't seem like a confrontation or a rapid-fire interrogation.

1.1 Enhancing Your Well-Being

In the modern world, it's important to take the time to uncover what makes you feel happy and successful. This will help with making choices that are more fulfilling and rejecting less fulfilling options. Other factors that contribute to well-being are feeling energetic and ready to take on life, and taking consistent action toward a healthy lifestyle. For some, well-being involves self-actualization, a term developed by Abraham Maslow, one of the leading humanistic psychologists of our time. Self-actualization refers to a progressive pursuit of growth and meaning in life.

1. Uncovering What Makes You Feel Happy and Successful

1. If you were charged with writing a happiness manifesto for yourself, what would it say?

2. Please tell me unapologetically and without guilt what an amazing life looks like for you.

3. Imagine you are eighty years old and looking back on your life, feeling satisfied with all you have done and who you have been. What does this life well lived look like?

4. Imagine your life story up until now was going to be published as a book. What would the title be? What would you like it to be?

5. Some people think, *I will be happy when...* If your credo was "Be Happy *Now*," what would you change?

6. The archetype of success is rich, famous, slim, and prestigious. What is your own view of success?

7. What do you want to change or give up, yet worry that if you do so, you will lose your footing and lose touch with who you are today?

8. Who inspires you? What does this say about your own wants and needs?

9. Why are you the luckiest person in the world?

10. When do you feel most satisfied and content?

11. What life changes would bring you more peace and ease?

12. When you connect to your soul, what is it longing for?

13. Who are the people that matter in your life, and what role would you like them to play in your life for the next decade?

14. What do you want to be fully present for in your life?

15. If you could give yourself the gift of time, how would you use it?

16. How do you define love? How might you expand love in your life?

17. What are you immensely grateful for right now?

18. What would it take for you to slow down and take pleasure in your precious days on earth?

2. Feeling Energetic and Ready to Take on Life

1. If you could completely revamp your life to be energizing, what would that life look like?

2. In your life, where is energy flowing? Where is it blocked?

3. Would you say you are honoring your ambition and drive without getting trapped by it? What changes would feel more energetic and freeing?

4. What is a work project that gives you energy the more you work on it?

5. In order for you to experience personal growth, where do you want to redirect your energy?

6. In order for you to feel more energetic, what needs to come off your plate?

7. Where are you on the burnout scale? High/medium/low?

8. What is making you grumpy?

9. Where is energy stuck in your body?

10. Who in your life is sucking your energy? Boosting it?

12. What is one new habit that would boost your energy?

13. What is something that sounds weird or a bit flaky but still may be worth trying in order to boost your energy?

14. How are emotions such as anger, grief, or jealousy impacting your energy?

3. Taking Care of Health

1. Based on your life right now, what might you die from?

2. When you look in the mirror, what do you see?

3. When you consider your health, what's working well? What positive lessons can you apply to other areas of your health regime?

4. Which of your health data is trending in the wrong direction?

5. What excuses are getting in the way of a healthier life?

6. What aspect of your health have you given up on?

7. In your view, what does it mean to age gracefully?

8. What does growing older feel like to you?

9. If you knew that in one year you would die suddenly, what would you change about the way you are living right now?

10. What is a thirty-day experiment you could embark on to improve your health?

11. Complete this sentence: If I brought 5 percent more conscious attention to my health, I would...

12. What would it take for you to feel younger next year?

4. Self-Actualization and Personal Growth as a Pathway to Well-Being

1. In your own words, how would you describe the difference between success and significance? How might you infuse more significance into your life?

2. What spiritual questions do you need answers to in order to self-actualize and grow as a person?

3. Are you aware of a spiritual dimension to your life? Would you like to deepen the spiritual connection in your life? If so, how?

4. What life story from your past is getting in the way of your self-actualization today? What will help you let go and rewrite the script?

5. What does it mean for you to be your most authentic self in your next life stage?

6. What new experiences or knowledge would help you evolve?

7. What life change would inspire you?

8. What is love? How can you invite more of it into your life?

9. What does community mean to you? What communities are you a part of? To what extent are these communities meeting your needs for personal growth and connection?

10. On a scale of one to five, how satisfying are your friendships?

11. Where would you like to be more mature in your dealings with others?

12. What is your relationship with money? How does this relationship impact your life?

13. Are you using social media as a tool for personal growth or to stunt your growth?

14. What is one of the best growth moments from your life that sucked at the time you were experiencing it?

15. How can you help others to grow and develop in their own lives?

16. How can you invite more awe and beauty into your life?

17. In your daily life, to what extent do you feel safe?

DUCK

Listening carefully and deeply to another person is one of the greatest gifts we can offer them.

1.2 Discovering Your Values

Discovering your values is the process of clarifying what is important to you. When you live your life according to your values, it feels that you are being true to yourself and true to what matters most to you. As you take action and design your life around your values, you will feel more fulfilled, although the path may not always be easy.

1. Clarifying What Is Important to You

1. What's most meaningful in your life?

2. What are your top ten values? What does each value mean to you?

3. Describe three fulfilling moments. What values do these moments have in common?

4. What values are so important to you that you are willing to endure some discomfort to pursue them? What values are so important to you that you are willing to deal with people treating you as an outcast or as a joke as you pursue them?

5. If you could go back in time and change one decision in your life, what decision would you change and why?

6. If today was your last day on earth, how would you make it count?

7. Complete this sentence: To live a life of no regrets means...

8. Have you ever hated anyone? If so, why? What values were being violated?

9. What's your favorite thing about being alive?

10. What is one thing you can't live without, and why?

11. If you had $1 million to donate to a cause that was important to you, what would you donate to, and why?

12. If you won $100 million and had to spend it in thirty days, what would you spend it on, and why?

13. What is something that is so important to you and so ingrained in the way you live your life that you don't even think about it, but the absence of which would make a profound difference to the quality of your life?

14. What are the things you make time for because you believe they are important for your survival? Any values you may be taking to the extreme here?

15. Finish this sentence: I wish I had more time for...

16. What's the most expensive thing you have ever paid for? Would you do it again?

17. What do you value about the country you live in?

18. What values are you absolutely not willing to compromise on?

19. What used to be important to you, yet no longer seems to be?

20. How are your values different from your parents'?

21. Other than accomplishing more, what will make you happy?

22. What are you becoming more aware of in your life?

23. What crushes your soul?

24. Where would you just love to get selfish?

25. What's the biggest mistake you have made in your life?

26. Have you ever been so happy you cried?

2. Designing a Life around Your Values

1. If you could imagine a values-oriented life, what would it look like?

2. Describe the perfect day.

3. To what extent are your values being expressed in your life right now?

4. Tell me about a time when you felt as if you did not honor your values. What was that like for you?

5. Guilt is often a clue that something is out of alignment between our values and actions. When do you experience guilt?

6. What are some of your regrets, and what have you learned from them that you can apply in the future?

7. Living a values-oriented life often has more to do with subtraction than addition. To live your values, what do you need to leave behind?

8. To live your values, what do you need to change or give up but worry that if you do, you will lose your edge and lose touch with who you are today?

9. Think of someone who inspires you. What values do you see as central to their life? How would your life be different if these same values were central to your life?

10. Compare different scenarios. Imagine your career was your top value. What would your life look like? Now imagine your family, spirit, giving back, and so forth, was your top value. Compare each scenario.

11. Which of your values tend to conflict with each other?

12. What do you feel you should want, yet you do not? What do you make of this incongruence?

13. If I told you this moment were a turning point, what do you imagine you'd be happy to be moving away from? Moving toward?

14. What are the signals you are getting that indicate it is time to live a more values-oriented existence?

15. How satisfied are you with the ways in which your values are integrated into your life? What are your doubts or worries when you consider integrating your values more fully?

16. What percentage of your weekly calendar appointments align with your values? Do you believe it possible to have greater alignment? What will it take?

17. When you imagine living your values, what are the competing tensions that may arise—for example, family versus work, self-interest versus family interest? How can you learn to deal with these tensions and thrive despite them?

18. If it were easy to live a values-oriented life, everyone would be doing it. What makes it challenging for you?

BUTTERFLY

If you ask someone a personal question, clarify whether the conversation is confidential. Baring your soul requires some safety.

1.3 Living on Purpose

One great question underlies the human experience: what is the purpose of life? Purpose is your reason for being. It's what gives you true happiness and a sense of contribution to the world. When you are making a difference and living with purpose, you feel congruent inside and out. Clarity of purpose often shifts over the course of our lifetimes: there are times when we feel lost and other times where we feel on track with our highest calling.

1. Identifying Your Reason for Being and Life Purpose

1. What are the unique gifts you bring to the world?

2. Why were you put on this earth?

3. Do you have an important message for the world? If so, what is it?

4. What's your reason for being?

5. Who are you? Who are you becoming?

6. What do you feel called to do?

7. Give me an example of a time in your life where you felt you were doing what you were meant to do.

8. Think of all your major life experiences (not just work). What's the thread that runs through them?

9. Tell me three stories that you believe reveal your destiny. Why these stories? What makes them significant to you?

10. If you believe in God or Spirit, what does this force most want for you?

11. Who are you? Who are you not?

12. You have achieved success. Now what?

13. If you were to die tomorrow, what three things would you NOT have accomplished that you wish you had?

14. What are the cries of the world that stir something within you?

15. What is the thing that pushes you out of the door day in and day out?

16. When you see yourself as interconnected with the whole universe, what stands out as important for you?

17. What was your dream as a child?

18. Consider your six greatest accomplishments to date. What was the motivation behind these accomplishments?

19. What gentle nudges does the universe keep giving you?

20. What kinds of things do people tend to ask you to do for them?

21. What transformation is waiting just around the corner for you?

22. Where do you sense you are being led to?

23. What does "living in your light" mean to you?

24. What inspires you about the future?

25. Where is your life's compass pointing to?

26. What if the purpose of life is to have fun?

2. Finding Ways to Make a Difference and Live Your Purpose

1. After you are gone, how will the world be different or better as a result of your life and contribution to the world?

2. What mark do you want to make with your life?

3. If you had a global platform to raise awareness about a vital issue, what issue would you choose?

4. How might you positively impact a million lives?

5. Are you doing what you're uniquely capable of— what you feel put on this earth to do?

6. What do you want to do regardless of whether you succeed or fail at it?

7. What gives you a deep sense of accomplishment?

8. In this world, where are you not replaceable?

9. What would feel worthwhile to do even if your efforts were rejected 150 times along the way?

10. What if purpose is more about *how* you do things than *what* things you do? What does this open up for you?

11. How can you use your strengths and gifts to serve the world?

12. Many people find their purpose during their darkest moments. How have your tragedies prepared you to serve?

13. What influences or events are leading you to believe that a new direction is in store for you?

14. What is getting in the way of fulfilling your life purpose?

15. To live your purpose, what's the blank slate you want to give yourself?

3. Clarifying Your Relationship with Purpose over Your Lifetime

1. Why does having a clear purpose matter to you?

2. To what extent are you clear on your purpose?

3. How has your purpose shifted over the course of your life?

4. What is clear about your purpose in this moment?

5. When did you feel lost in your life?

6. In one sentence, how would you describe your purpose today?

1.4 Finding a Meaningful Career Path

Creating a meaningful career path begins with looking back and taking an inventory of your career history so that you can evaluate peak moments as well as when you felt off track. It also involves setting a personal vision and exploring passions, preferences, and strengths. Ultimately, though, it's important to take action toward your chosen career path so that you can experiment and see what actually works well day to day.

1. Exploring Your Career History to Find Nuggets of Fulfillment

1. What successes have you already had in your career that you would like to take to the next level?

2. What are the top five choices that brought your career to where it is today?

3. What are the peaks and valleys of your career so far?

4. Describe five situations from your career where you felt in the flow. What are the themes that run through these experiences?

5. What has been the peak of your career so far? How can you ensure there is another peak?

6. What have been some of your soul-crushing work moments?

7. In what ways has your career had a life of its own?

8. What are the serendipities that got you to where you are today?

9. What feels stale in your career? What is something you have outgrown?

10. What's the mark you want to make in your current career before you move on?

11. How will you know it's time to make a career change?

12. If you go through a career change, what are two things that you want to remain stable?

2. Setting a Career Direction That Is Fulfilling and Gratifying

1. In your work, do you feel driven or called? What's the difference between a career and a calling?

2. What is the greatest vision you have for your career?

3. Imagine you are ten years older and pleased with the contributions you have made in your career. What have you achieved?

4. Imagine it is ten years from now and your career is mediocre. Would that matter to you?

5. What are you passionate about?

6. What are five careers that appeal to you, and why?

7. What do you want to be when you grow up?

8. What are your strengths, gifts, and interests?

9. What would you do (or not do) if money weren't a factor?

10. What career possibilities are opening up for you right now?

11. What do you love to do that you could charge money for?

12. What kinds of companies are looking for people like you?

13. What are the key words you would like to use to describe your career in five years? In one year?

14. If you were held captive and had to make $5 million in six months doing something you enjoyed, what would you focus on?

15. If you had $100,000 to invest in a start-up, what kind of business would you invest in?

16. What if instead of working forty-nine weeks a year with a three-week vacation, you could work three weeks per year with a forty-nine-week vacation? What are ten crazy ideas for making this a reality?

17. Often when we think of our career vision, we imagine what we are doing or what we will accomplish. Consider this differently. What we want to do is simply find a way to achieve a state of being. Make a list of what you want to do, and then ask yourself: if you do this, what state of being do you hope to achieve?

18. Who do you aspire to be?

3. Defining Your Work Preferences

1. What would a perfect week look like for you? Whom would you be working with? What hours would you work? What type of work would you be doing?

2. What would an ideal year look like for you?

3. What criteria are you using to evaluate whether a career is a good fit for you?

4. What career paths are you glorifying?

5. What does success mean to you?

6. How much money do you need? How much do you want?

7. What's a good work pace for you? How much pressure seems appropriate?

8. What career options align with who you want to be as a parent?

9. What does work-life integration mean to you?

10. What is the ideal work culture for you?

11. When making career choices, how important is flexibility/control over how you spend your time?

12. What career options might give you time and control over your schedule instead of someone else calling the shots for you?

13. What industries fascinate you? Interest you?

14. What character traits do you value in your work colleagues?

15. What do you want to say no to in your career?

16. Who has your dream career?

4. Identifying and Developing Your Strengths

1. Where do you have the potential to shine on the world stage?

2. In your field, what separates average performers from the stars?

3. In your field, what makes you uncommon? How can you become unique?

4. What are two or three things you are really good at and you enjoy doing?

5. In what aspects of your field do you have the greatest expertise?

6. What skills are you inspired to develop?

7. What are some activities that engage you so fully that you lose track of time?

8. Ask five of your colleagues, "What do you see as my unique talents, skills, and abilities?"

5. Taking Action toward a Fulfilling Career

1. How can you test a career path to see if it's right for you?

2. If you had to launch a new career in the next twenty-four hours, how might you do it?

3. What's a little career experiment you could try?

4. What's the best way to gain experience in your chosen field?

5. Career experts talk about getting started on a career path by starting a parallel career—that is, a career that runs parallel to your current career path and builds over time. What is a parallel career that will set you up for the long term?

6. Who can help you achieve your career goals?

7. How will you know your career is on track?

8. What's the first step?

DUCK
Remember: It takes a great deal of courage to answer a powerful question.

1.5 Setting Personal Goals

Setting goals starts with identifying what you want and evaluating the opportunities before you. When your goals align with your values, this can stack the odds of success in your favor. When establishing goals, it's valuable to consider how you want to feel as you strive to achieve them and what you would like the process to be like. And, of course, concrete goals include action steps, strategies for overcoming constraints and obstacles, and ways to measure success.

1. Identifying What You Want to Achieve

1. What are the juiciest opportunities in front of you right now?

2. What's the big win you are after?

3. What are three things you want to achieve, and why?

4. What are your most important goals?

5. What would be a huge and seemingly insurmountable challenge that would be fun to surpass?

6. If you were ten times bolder with your goals, what would you strive for?

7. What if you had to pick just one goal? What would it be, and why?

8. What goals speak to your heart?

9. What are three scenarios that would be acceptable for you to achieve?

10. We live in a world of exponential change. To what extent is this reflected in your goals?

2. Taking Action toward Your Goals

1. What exactly do you want to accomplish, and by when?

2. What are your must do's, and what are the nice to do's?

3. What's the first step toward achieving your goal?

4. When pursuing a key goal, what will stack the odds of success in your favor?

5. To best achieve this goal, what do you need to accept fully about the present reality?

6. What if you gave yourself thirty years to achieve this goal? What might change in your approach? What if you gave yourself three months?

7. What other priorities will compete with achieving this goal?

8. Who has already achieved something similar? What can you learn from them?

9. What are the regular habits that will move you toward your goal?

3. Exploring the Link between Goals, Values, and Feelings

1. Why is this goal important to you?

2. How will you live your values and achieve this goal?

3. Which of your values may get sidelined if you go for this goal?

4. How do you want to feel as you achieve this goal?

5. What's the most comfortable and manageable way to achieve this goal?

6. If you could wave your magic wand and have the journey be fun, what would that look like?

7. On a scale of 0 to 100 percent, how committed are you?

4. Identifying Constraints and Obstacles Related to Goals

1. Let's assume you are going to be superbusy and distracted as you strive to achieve this goal. What systems do you need to put in place to make sure you follow through?

2. When was the last time you claimed you were going to do something and didn't follow through at the level you'd hoped? How can you avoid doing this now?

3. Let's imagine you have already achieved your goal. Not once but twice. How might you tackle it the third time around, with some experience under your belt?

4. If you don't achieve this goal, will this really matter five or ten years from now?

5. What might get in the way of your success?

6. What might prevent you from going all in?

7. Can you anticipate any downsides to achieving this goal?

8. What constraints will you need to work around?

9. How might your attitude get in the way of your success?

10. What excuses may prevent you from achieving this goal?

11. Once you start on the path of achieving this goal, will turning back be an option for you?

12. If you are going to pursue this goal, what do you need to say no to?

13. Quitting things that don't work can be integral to success. What are the signs that you may need to cut your losses and pursue something different?

14. When you fail to achieve your goals, what excuses do you tend to make privately?

5. Measuring Success and Goal Outcomes

1. A year from now, what do you want to be celebrating?

2. As it relates to your goals, what does excellence mean to you?

3. What's the minimum standard you are after?

4. As you strive to achieve your goal, what's the most probable outcome?

5. What is a stretch target?

6. Have you ever put a limit on yourself, only to surpass it? What did that teach you about goal setting?

7. How will you know you have successfully achieved your goal? What metric will you pay attention to?

8. What's a completely subjective measurement that is appropriate for assessing your achievements?

9. What distinguishes stellar performance from mediocre performance in this area?

10. How will your life be different if you achieve this goal? Other people's lives?

11. If you achieve this goal, what opportunities may open up for you?

12. What technology can help you measure and track your progress?

13. When you achieve this goal, how do you want to celebrate?

BUTTERFLY

Transformational coaching requires some silence. This allows others to pay attention to what they are experiencing and creates space for reflection.

1.6 Building Confidence

Exploring what makes you feel confident and what evokes insecurity is a valuable exercise for self-awareness. For most people, confidence is contextual, meaning that some situations feel comfortable and others do not. When in a situation marked by insecurity, it can be helpful to pause and explore how fear and worry may take over your thoughts and to evaluate whether your mind is dwelling on the worst-case scenario. Building confidence requires a positive mindset and self-trust, and the overarching belief that you have the ability to size up a situation adequately and to do what is best given the circumstances.

1. Exploring Confidence and What It Means

1. Have you ever thought about these words: self-esteem, confidence, motivation? What do they mean to you? How are they connected and distinct from one another?

2. In your view, what's the connection between confidence, risk, and failure? How has this manifested in your life and/or career?

3. According to Nathaniel Branden, the late psychotherapist best known for his work on confidence and self-esteem, confidence arises when we trust ourselves to size up a situation and do what is best given the circumstances. Can you trust yourself to size up a situation and do what is best given the circumstances? Why, or why not?

4. Confidence often comes from knowing a subject, being prepared, and being in a context or situation with which we are familiar. Who or what helps you to feel confident?

5. One perspective is that confidence comes from knowing that suffering, failure, and rejection are inevitable in life. How could your pain also be a tool for your progress?

6. Some people believe confidence is a skill. What about you?

7. Confidence can be derailed by certain circumstances or people. Who or what derails your confidence?

8. Confidence is sometimes described as feeling sure of yourself. Would you say you are generally a confident person? Why, or why not?

9. How would you define confidence? In your life so far, what is your experience of confidence?

10. In your view, how important is confidence for your success and well-being? What is the relationship between these concepts in your life?

11. Confidence is a complicated subject. What's complicated about confidence for you?

2. Assessing and Building Confidence in a Given Situation

1. On a scale of one to five, how confident are you in your ability to handle this situation?

2. In this situation, what is getting in the way of fully trusting yourself?

3. Tell me about a time when you were brave. How can you awaken your bravery now?

4. I believe you can do this. Let me tell you why. Why do you believe in yourself?

5. In what ways are you overestimating others and underestimating yourself?

6. To what extent are you being impacted by people's potential criticism of you? Does every person's criticism affect you in the same way?

7. If you view yourself as a constant "work in progress," does anything shift for you?

8. What will it take for you to win and experience success?

3. Overcoming Fear When Feeling Insecure

1. What fears or worries do you need to overcome to feel more confident?

2. On a scale of one to five, how intense is your fear?

3. If you could lock your fear in a room for good, what would be left?

4. If your fears or worries had a voice, whose voice would it sound like?

5. Where do you feel fear in your body?

6. When negative emotions take over, how do you reconnect with your center?

7. Tell me about a courage moment—a moment where you felt the fear and did it anyway.

8. If you had a year to live, would this concern you?

9. It's common to feel alone in our fears. When you consider your fears, how might they be part of a universal experience impacting all of humanity?

10. Tell me about three situations in which you felt confidence. How could you tap into some of that confidence now?

4. Managing the Worst-Case Scenario in a Given Situation

1. What's the worst that can happen?

2. How probable is the worst-case scenario?

3. If the worst-case scenario did happen, how might you handle it?

4. What's rejection like for you?

5. What if you get laughed out of the room? Then what?

6. What's exciting about rejection?

7. What if you lost everything in your life and had to rebuild it in six months? How would you do it?

5. Building Confidence in a Given Situation

1. What is the role you have played in all of your successes so far? How can you tap into your strengths now?

2. In this situation, how can you add value?

3. Why are you the best person to handle this situation?

4. What are five things that are awesome about you? How can you tap into these strengths?

5. Who do you need to become to rise to this challenge?

6. What's your confidence ritual?

7. It's hard to feel confident if you are not prepared. To feel confident, what do you need to do to prepare?

8. What does this quote mean to you?

"A journey of a thousand miles starts with a single step."

—Lao-tzu

9. What are your biggest insecurities? How might you overcome each one?

10. Why do you belong with this crowd?

11. What assistance do you need to feel more confident?

12. What's your power pose (a body posture that helps you feel confident)?

13. What risks are you willing to take?

14. What courage would you like to muster?

1.7 Shifting Mindset and Beliefs

Your mindset is your attitude and the way you perceive things—the lens through which you view things in the world. Shifting your mindset begins with self-awareness about your thinking habits and being deliberate about shifting your perspective when your mental chatter is unproductive. Changing your mindset involves changing your self-talk, cultivating practices to calm your mind, and updating your core beliefs. As you become more aware of your thoughts, the way you see the world may start to shift as well.

1. Exploring an Individual's General Mindset

1. On a scale of one to five (five is optimal), how is your typical mindset?

2. What circumstances automatically ruin your mood?

3. When your thoughts wander, where do they go?

4. What dualities (black/white, good/bad) are alive and well in your thinking?

5. Do you tend to focus on the positive or the negative aspects of a given situation?

6. How is technology hijacking your mind?

7. What pushes your buttons?

8. What are the habitual thoughts that contribute to your successes?

9. If your inner judge had a persona, what would it be?

10. In what ways is your thinking still in the dark ages?

11. What's the relationship between your mental attitude and physical fitness?

2. Exploring Mindset in a Given Situation

1. Tell me about your self-talk.

2. On a scale of one to five, how loud is your internal chatter?

3. What thoughts are empowering you?

4. What is your internal judge saying?

5. Which voice in your head is speaking the loudest—the empowering one or the judge?

6. What are you ignoring or failing to see?

7. What are you minimizing?

8. What are you catastrophizing?

3. Shifting Mindset and Perspective in a Given Situation

1. Imagine this situation is preparing you for what you were put on this planet to do. How does that change your perspective?

2. If you are effective at navigating this situation, what might the impact be on your career, friends, and/or family?

3. If you approached your situation like a Navy SEAL, what would be different about your thinking?

4. If you approached your situation like a Zen master, what would be different about your thinking?

5. Warriors are people who are attracted to a challenge. They gain fulfillment from conquering a challenge and experiencing victory. In what areas of your life would you like to awaken your inner warrior?

6. How would someone with an abundance mindset think in this situation?

7. What's the optimistic view of this situation?

8. Imagine it's ten years into the future, and this situation has turned out well. What thinking contributed to your success?

9. What helps you slow down the chatter in your mind?

10. How might you reset yourself so you can think more clearly?

4. Exploring and Changing Core Beliefs

1. What are your beliefs about money/love/success/control?

2. Which of these beliefs are limiting or out of date?

3. Complete this sentence: I don't have X because...

4. Complete this sentence: I would love to have more of X, but...

5. Fill in the blank: If I succeed, _____ will happen.

6. Fill in the blank: If I fail, _____ will happen.

7. Fill in the blank: The good and bad things that happen to me are the result of _____.

8. What limiting beliefs have you changed in your life so far? How did you change them?

9. Why do you believe [insert any belief that shapes your current thinking]?

10. Where do you think you will be in a few years if you keep hanging on to this belief?

11. What evidence is there that this belief is true?

12. What evidence is there that this belief may not be true?

13. What's a new belief that is different from your current belief but equally plausible?

14. What's the opposite belief to the one you hold?

15. What would it take for you to change your belief?

16. What is going to improve if you adopt a new belief?

17. How can you keep this new belief fresh in your mind?

5. Exploring Paradigms That Impact Thinking Patterns and Mindset

1. The word paradigm refers to the conceptual framework, belief system, and overall perspective through which you see and interpret the world. What are the roots of your current prevailing paradigm?

2. How do you see your prevailing paradigm impacting your current reality?

3. How does your prevailing paradigm affect and limit what you see and know?

4. What other paradigms are equally valid and/or are you curious about?

5. When has your worldview been radically expanded or altered?

6. What are you curious to learn about or experience in order to expand your worldview?

BUTTERFLY

A coach is an advocate for another person, reminding them that someone is on their side.

1.8 Making Decisions

A decision can change the course of your life, so it's wise to be thoughtful when making important decisions. When making decisions, it is valuable to generate lots of options to choose from, weigh your choices carefully, and consider how your choices will impact your values and contribute to your fulfillment. Having said that, sometimes it's best to just go for it, recognizing that taking no action may lead to regret.

1. Generating Options in a Specific Situation

1. What are five options you could consider?

2. What are some unconventional options?

3. What option would be the most fulfilling for you?

4. What options deeply resonate with you?

5. Choosing between two things often doesn't feel like a true choice. Is there a third or fourth option?

6. What is an option that is so obvious you may have overlooked it?

7. What if you do nothing?

8. When generating options, what self-imposed limits are getting in the way?

2. Weighing Options in a Specific Situation

1. Which option best aligns with your purpose and mission in life?

2. Which option would be enjoyable to pursue today and benefit you in the future?

3. My philosophy is that if the options available to you don't cause harm to yourself and others, you can go with the option that feels the best. When you consider the options available to you, do any of them cause harm to you and others? Which option feels best?

4. What would be the impact of each option on your family?

5. Do you feel any external pressures to go with one option over another?

6. What option best fits with your personal values?

7. Is there an option that you know in your heart you should take, but you are afraid to pull the trigger? In the depths of your subconscious, do you know exactly what you should do, but you can't muster the strength or courage to do it?

8. What if a spiritual master were making the same decision you are facing. What might he or she decide? What would a Martian decide? Your mother?

9. What choice would your wise self like to make?

10. What "great opportunity" ultimately feels like the "wrong opportunity" for you?

11. What are the messages you are getting about this issue from society at large? How are these messages influencing how you think about your options?

12. What would your parents say about the options you are considering?

13. When you consider each option, what are your hopes and fears?

3. Making a Choice in a Specific Situation

1. What are your top three criteria for making this choice?

2. With this choice, are you playing to win or playing not to lose?

3. What are the tensions or competing values that are evident in this choice?

4. What are the constraints that are important to consider?

5. What research do you need to do in order to make an effective decision?

6. With these options, is there anything you can do to maximize the upside? Minimize the downside?

7. Could you be overstating the benefits of any of the options? The disadvantages?

8. When making this decision, are you sitting on the fence? What's it like to be on the fence?

9. What is a non-negotiable must-have?

10. What trade-offs seem reasonable?

11. Can this decision wait? What are the implications of putting this decision on hold?

12. If you took no action, what regrets might you have?

13. If your decision doesn't work out, then what?

14. What's your decision-making process?

Section 2

LEADING OTHERS

Talent wins games, but teamwork and
intelligence wins championships.
—*Michael Jordan*

If you are like most leaders, you are often asked to wear the "coach hat" in your day-to-day work. The questions in this section will help you to coach others on common leadership topics that you will inevitably face. Topics include building a high-performing team, developing leadership potential, delegating, and becoming more influential.

On a personal note, this section is near and dear to my heart. As an executive coach, I use these questions all the time. I wish I'd had them earlier in my career! I would have avoided some embarrassing moments when I felt stuck, unsure what questions to ask a client.

For example, early in my career I was coaching the chief technology officer of an international technology company. He characterized himself as a technical geek who struggled to influence the CEO on the company's strategic technology agenda. In one of our coaching sessions, he described feeling stressed and pressured. He said, "Help me! I can't get the CEO to do what I need him to do, and if I don't resolve this, I am going to quit!" I tried a number of different approaches to get at the root of the problem, but I just couldn't seem to get to the heart of the matter. As the session went on, I felt a looming feeling of incompetence. I thought, *Yikes! What should I ask here?* Looking back, I needed better questions on how to align stakeholders around a common agenda and how to create win-win agreements. It would have been helpful also to explore the client's mindset, confidence, and core beliefs. The questions in this section would have been invaluable to me.

Although I managed to fumble my way through the coaching session (and somehow managed to keep the client), I wouldn't want you to experience that awkwardness. Read this section carefully, and use the questions to help others to succeed.

2. Leading Others

DUCK

True listening is active and engaged. It is more about offering questions than giving answers.

BUTTERFLY

Don't let your ego get in the way when you are asking questions. Remember: The point of asking questions is not for you to be brilliant. It's for those answering the questions to be brilliant.

2.1 Building a High-Performance Team

Being on a top-performing team is one of the best feelings in the world. High-performing teams have a purpose, shared values, a clear direction, and goal. The best teams are productive and have a positive team dynamic. Team members trust one another and work through conflicts constructively.

1. Uncovering Team Purpose and Values

1. Why does this team exist?

2. What does this team want to do that it has not done yet?

3. What legacy does this team want to leave behind?

4. Why is this team successful?

5. What unites this team other than the work that you do together?

6. What does this team value? Why are its values important?

7. What does this team stand for?

8. What is the unique value this team brings to the organization?

9. If this team were a famous brand, what brand would it be, and why?

10. What does this team want to be known for?

11. What's the team's personality?

12. What do you treasure about this team?

13. In three words, describe this team today. In the near future, what three words do you hope will describe this team?

14. What do other teams in the organization tend to say about this team?

15. What are the lessons or stories from the past that have shaped who this team is today?

16. How are the values of this team communicated to others?

17. What impact would it have on the organization if they knew what was important to this team?

18. What are the signature stories that communicate what matters to this team?

19. Is having a team identity important to this team? Why, or why not?

2. Establishing Team Goals

1. What big opportunities are before this team?

2. What are the long-, medium-, and short-term goals for this team?

3. What is going to be the biggest leadership challenge facing this team in the next few years?

4. What do the team's stakeholders (customers, employees) need this team to step up and do?

5. What accomplishment would make this the team's most memorable year yet?

6. Have each team member finish this sentence: An extraordinary goal for this team would be...

7. What's the greatest contribution this team wants to make to the organization?

8. What does this team want to be celebrating one year from now?

9. When you look at this team's goals, what's the elephant in the room that is holding the team back from achieving its goals?

10. What does this team want to do that it hasn't done yet? Why hasn't it?

11. What is this team not even attempting because it is too hard, or because members fear failure?

12. What are the key performance indicators that matter to this team?

13. What's happening in the larger context (economy/industry/region) that may impact the future of this team?

3. Establishing and Managing Team Agreements

1. What team agreements does this team need to put in place to be more effective?

2. What are the behaviors that support each of the team's agreements?

3. What are the unspoken agreements on this team?

4. Complete this sentence: On this team, I assume that if _____ happens, then _____ will happen.

5. When team agreements are not met, how would the team like to handle it?

6. What are the different ways team members are provided with feedback about their contributions?

7. When should someone be asked to leave this team?

4. Improving Team Productivity and Results

1. What is the evidence that this team has the potential to excel?

2. What results would set this team apart in the industry?

3. As a team, are you going for ordinary or extraordinary results?

4. What would help improve the team's productivity?

5. What are the regular team practices that would help the team achieve results?

6. What are the regular team habits undermining this team's performance?

7. To be more productive, what's the most important investment this team needs to make?

8. What are the quick wins this team wants to pursue?

9. What is urgent for this team to do?

10. What is important, yet not urgent?

11. Would you say this team is overcommitted? Why, or why not?

12. What skill development would help this team excel?

13. How do team members know that they're becoming more effective?

14. What is one thing that would dramatically improve team meetings?

15. How can this team do a better job of managing available resources?

16. Does the team have the right skills and roles in place?

17. Which systems or rituals would help this team stay focused on what matters?

18. Where has this team inadvertently dropped its standards?

19. What is the team's history of assimilating new team members? What has been the impact of this approach?

20. What does this team talk about but fail to follow through on?

21. Where is the team's commitment wavering?

22. What enables or inhibits the team's decision making?

23. In your view, what's the relationship between this team's culture and its productivity?

5. Improving Team Dynamics and Teamwork

1. What does teamwork mean to you?

2. How do you feel about this team's future?

3. What is getting in the way of the team's success? Why does the team tolerate it? For what purpose?

4. Ask each team member: What is a challenge you are facing? What do you need from this team to succeed?

5. What emotions do you feel are inappropriate to express on this team?

6. What conflicting messages do you experience on this team?

7. Would you say members of this team look out for one another? Why, or why not?

8. Describe a dysfunctional team you've been a member of. How is your current team behaving like that dysfunctional team?

9. How does this team tend to behave when things get difficult?

10. Imagine this team meeting went viral on YouTube. What would others see? What do you want them to see?

11. What would this team do differently if it were an all-star team?

12. When this team looks at current models of high-performing teams, do those models seem to represent this team's truth and aspirations?

13. What is happening on this team that impacts the organization as a whole?

14. Ask each team member: in what ways is this team a vehicle for your own growth as a leader?

15. What would help this team feel more connected and more resilient?

16. What is challenging about being on this team?

17. How does this team compare to other teams you have been on?

18. Where does competition show up on this team?

19. Where is this team absolutely aligned?

20. What's undermining this team's success?

21. What's taboo on this team?

22. What quality of this team would the team be disappointed to see emulated in other teams?

23. What's a metaphor that describes where this team is now? Where the team wants to be?

24. What's your worst team habit? Best?

25. Describe the perfect team meeting.

26. In what ways is the team's drive for results negatively impacting the team dynamic?

27. Looking back, what stressors from the past have weakened the team? What stressors have strengthened it?

28. If the team improves its dynamics, what business outcomes would also likely improve?

6. Enhancing Trust and Constructively Handling Conflicts

1. Have each team member finish this sentence: If you really knew me, you would know...

2. How comfortable is this group with conflict? Do the team members tend to have honest dialogue about issues, or not express concerns?

3. What helps to build trust on this team? Erodes it?

4. What does true cooperation feel like? When was the last time you experienced this on the team?

5. What is the truth this team needs to hear?

6. What is the hardest part of being on this team?

7. What's the difference between a heated conversation and a toxic conversation?

8. If two people are upset with each other, how does it play out in the team?

9. What behaviors show up on this team when team members are anxious?

10. When there is stress or tension on the team, how does it impact the organization as a whole?

11. How do team members determine what is appropriate to discuss within the team?

12. If this team viewed conflict as an opportunity to invest in relationships, what would change in the team dynamic?

13. What's getting in the way of open, honest conversations on the team?

14. What are the limits of team harmony?

15. What's the elephant in the room?

16. What conversation is the team avoiding?

17. What would help this team get better at challenging one another's thinking?

18. What would help this team resolve conflicts quicker?

19. To be a more cohesive team, what does this team need to unlearn? Learn?

20. Where is this team lacking diversity, and why?

21. What are some voices on this team that need to be heard?

22. In what ways is this team too homogeneous in its thinking?

DUCK

Coaching helps us to listen to what is really going on. Notice more than the words: the energy, the pauses, the passion, the body.

2.2 Enhancing Leadership Style

Becoming a better leader is an endless pursuit. When first becoming a leader and during career transitions, it is valuable for leaders to identify their principles and leadership philosophy—what they value and stand for as leaders, and what leadership means to them.

As a leader, it is important to refine one's style continuously in order to bring out the best in others and shape the future. Developing as a leader requires continued personal growth and self-awareness. Moreover, when leaders are in an environment that supports their growth, this helps to nudge them along their leadership development path.

1. Identifying Your Leadership Principles

1. What do you want to be known for as a leader?

2. How do you want people to feel when they engage with you?

3. What do you stand for as a leader? Is this obvious to others?

4. What famous leader do you most identify with or admire?

5. What do you have in common with some of the great leaders of our time?

6. As a leader, what are you obsessed with?

7. What is one leadership principle that you would like to be central to your personal brand as a leader?

8. Draw a picture: As a leader, who are you now? Who are you becoming?

2. Exploring Leadership Philosophy

1. Some say leaders are "brokers of hope." What does this mean to you?

2. As a leader, how do you influence people's lives for the better?

3. In your view, what is the essence of leadership?

4. In your view, what distinguishes the best leaders from the rest?

5. What's changing about the world of work? What might this mean for how you need to lead in the future?

6. What have your kids taught you about leadership?

7. Would you say leadership is a job or a calling?

8. How have you seen the best leaders balance authenticity with diplomacy? How are you at striking this balance?

9. In your view, when is it important to show strength as a leader, and when is it important to show vulnerability?

10. What positive lessons are you learning about leadership from Millennials?

11. In your view, what is the link between a person's spiritual journey and his or her growth as a leader?

3. Refining Your Leadership Style

1. What three words would people use to describe your leadership style?

2. Who is a leader who inspires you? What qualities does he or she have that you would like to cultivate?

3. What clues are you getting that your leadership style needs an update?

4. Under what circumstances do you feel you need to be more effective at adapting your leadership style?

5. What's your worst "boss horror story"? How are you like that boss sometimes?

6. Have you ever received feedback about your leadership style that surprised you?

7. Have you received similar feedback more than once?

8. What feedback have you received about your leadership style that you know also applies to your personal life?

9. What steps have you taken to understand your strengths as a leader? What are your strengths?

10. Some say weaknesses are overused strengths. Would you say this is true for you?

11. How might your leadership style be contributing to or stunting innovation and growth?

12. Regardless of your gender, how might "feminine values" give your leadership style an edge?

4. Developing as a Leader

1. What have you done recently to increase your self-awareness?

2. Where do you want to be more mature in your dealings with others?

3. Complete this sentence: My ego is getting in the way of my leadership by...

4. How have you grown as a leader over the years?

5. What is the personal growth that will lead to your leadership growth?

6. There is a saying that the minute leaders don't want power, they have lots of it. How does this fit with your experience?

7. Would you say being a leader is part of your personal identity?

8. Leaders tend to get criticized. What worries you about this possibility?

9. What has been your toughest leadership moment?

10. Consider the people on your team. What does each of them need most from you? How do you know?

11. If I were to ask your team about your key areas that could use development, what do you think they might say?

12. As a leader, how might your areas for development actually be an asset?

13. What process might help you get a better understanding of your leadership growth areas?

14. How motivated are you to evolve as a leader?

15. To evolve as a leader, how does your relationship with yourself need to evolve?

16. What is your leadership development plan?

5. Exploring a Leader's Environment

1. When you look around the organization, which leaders tend to succeed and why?

2. What are the obstacles in this organization for aspiring leaders?

3. What are the barriers for women and minorities who aspire to leadership roles?

4. Would you say there is a glass ceiling in this organization?

5. In this organization, what steps are being taken to develop the next generation of leaders?

6. Who is your successor?

7. If you won the lotto tomorrow, who could step in and perform your role?

BUTTERFLY

The word courage comes from the Latin cor, which literally means heart. When you ask a question, recognize that it is an opportunity for someone to tap into and acknowledge their heart—an act of courage.

2.3 Coaching High-Potential Talent

High-potential employees tend to see challenge as a growth opportunity, and they are willing to put in discretionary effort. They are like gardens—worth tending to so that you can watch them bloom year after year.

When coaching high-potential talent, it's valuable to ask questions related to their career aspirations—how they want to develop their skills and what motivates them—so that you can craft job assignments that will unleash their potential. It's also important to have regular personal check-ins so that you are not blindsided by unexplored issues that may impact your direct reports.

1. Exploring Career Aspirations with High-Potential Talent

1. What are your career goals?

2. Why did you become [insert profession]?

3. Where do you see yourself five years from now?

4. What meaningful contribution would you like to make in this company?

5. How does this job fit into a broader career or life plan for you?

6. At this stage in your life, what does success mean to you?

7. From a career perspective, what would make your heart sing?

8. How do you want to make a difference in your field or industry?

9. Whose career would you like to emulate, and why?

10. In your career, what legacy do you hope to leave?

11. In your professional life, in what ways do you repeatedly undermine yourself and move away from your best, risk-tolerant self?

12. Where do you feel stuck in your professional life?

13. Do you feel that your role is a good fit for you?

14. What parts of your career and/or role have you outgrown?

15. Would you say you are a high potential employee? Why, or why not?

16. What's your five-year career plan?

17. What's a wild card that could disrupt your career plan?

18. What may be blocking your professional growth?

19. As you go for your career goals, what competition do you expect? How might you deal with this?

2. Finding Opportunities for Skill Development

1. What distinguishes top performers in your field?

2. How are you future-proofing your career (developing skills that will be relevant in the future world of work)?

3. What are the mistakes you have seen others consistently make in your field that you would like to avoid?

4. What could you learn this year that would benefit the rest of your career?

5. What do you need to learn to drive massive change in this business?

6. What challenging assignment would help you rapidly compress your learning and professional growth?

7. How can you get yourself connected to a broader, more diverse, professional network?

8. What's something you want to get really good at?

9. What projects might benefit from your skill set?

10. When you think about the future, where will you add the most value to the company?

11. What's something you are not qualified to do but motivated to try?

12. Do you feel this company is really using your talents?

13. How can the company get a better return on your time?

14. During what percentage of your time do you believe you are operating out of your strengths?

15. What's more valuable to you—increasing the depth of your skill set or widening its breadth?

16. What's the same/different about your skills this year compared to last year? What would you like to be same/different a year from now?

17. Stress is inherent in most successful careers. How can you become better at letting go of tension?

18. What have you learned recently that you would like to teach others?

19. Who would be a good mentor for you?

20. What can we do to increase your exposure to key people?

21. What kind of coaching would you benefit from?

22. What learning goal would be meaningful but also put you out of your comfort zone?

23. What feedback would be helpful for you?

24. What is something small you can do every day to help you realize your potential?

3. Uncovering Motivations and Interests

1. What excites you about this business?

2. What aspects of your work are you most passionate about?

3. What are the goals that matter most to you?

4. Where are you striving for excellence, and why?

5. What's your Picasso (that piece of work you are motivated to make a work of art)?

6. What do you love about your job?

7. If you were to receive an award this year, what award would mean something to you?

8. What do you see as your boss' priorities? How do you want to contribute here?

9. How do you like to be appreciated?

10. What is feeling stale in your career?

11. Is there any career interest you have yet feel afraid to try?

12. Ideally, what would you like to get off your plate?

13. What are the most/least rewarding parts of your job?

14. How motivated are you to put in extra effort?

15. When was the last time you googled yourself? Would you say your online reputation reflects your career aspirations?

16. What are you keen to start doing? Stop doing?

17. What were your highs and lows since we last met?

18. What attracted you to this company?

19. Would you pick this job if you could do it again?

20. Hindsight is 20/20. What do you wish you'd known when you first took this job?

21. How motivated are you to stay with this organization?

22. What kind of opportunity might entice you to leave this business?

4. Checking in with High-Potential Talent in Meaningful Ways

1. What's the most significant thing that has happened to you since we last met?

2. What were the moments of truth or critical decisions you made this last year?

3. If you could wave your magic wand and improve your day-to-day life, what would you change, and why?

4. What are your big ideas?

5. Would you say you are making progress on your top goals?

6. What challenges or obstacles are you facing right now?

7. What can we focus on today that will help you leapfrog your results?

8. How are you feeling about things these days?

9. What's on your mind lately?

10. How can I help you succeed?

11. What are you loving about work right now?

12. Where are you feeling stuck?

13. Anything niggling at you?

14. What's interfering with your growth as a professional/leader?

15. What books, websites, podcasts, and/or people are helping you stay inspired?

16. What's sapping your energy?

17. What feedback would be helpful for you?

18. What is one small adjustment we can make in this company that would make a positive difference for you?

19. Is there anything happening outside of work that you want me to be aware of?

20. Where do you need my executive sponsorship?

21. I would like to better support your career growth. Any advice on how to do this?

22. Is there any question I should have asked you but didn't?

23. What else would you like to talk about?

DUCK

When asking questions, listen from a place of compassion, not judgment.

2.4 Influencing Others

To be more influential, it's important to be clear about **what** you are trying to influence and **whom** you would like to influence. Be explicit about your influence goal and knowledgeable about who your stakeholders truly are, with their respective needs and unique motivations. This will enable you to craft your message and choose strategies that will influence your stakeholders to take actions that support your goals. Effective influencing is a high-integrity process that looks for win-win solutions.

1. Clarifying Your Influence Goal

1. What do you want to influence? What's your goal?

2. Why is this important to you?

3. What are the little goals that will support your big goals?

4. If you achieve your goal, what's the benefit to your stakeholders?

5. If you achieve your goal, who might lose out?

6. What resources do you need to achieve your goal?

7. If you could wave your magic wand and have your pursuit of this goal unfold perfectly, what would that look like?

8. If you are successful, what impact will it have on the future of this business? On your career?

2. Assessing Your Stakeholders

1. To achieve this goal, whom do you need on board?

2. Would you say your stakeholders care about your goal? Why, or why not?

3. What might get in the way of your ability to influence your stakeholders?

4. How will you convince your stakeholders it is worthwhile for them to invest their time and energy toward your goal?

5. Who will advocate for your goal, reinforcing that it is a good idea and worthy of time and energy?

6. Who will resist it?

7. Who will be sitting on the fence?

8. Good ideas are shot down all the time. What will you do if (and when) yours is shot down?

9. If you were in any of your stakeholder's shoes, why might you say no?

10. Who will be easy to influence, just because they like you?

11. On a scale of one to five, how much do your stakeholders trust you?

12. What's the correlation between the quality of your relationships with each stakeholder and your ability to influence them?

13. What's going on inside you when you interact with your key stakeholders?

14. Consider each of your stakeholders. What's their personal agenda, and how might it impact your ability to influence them?

3. Picking the Best Influence Tactic and Style

1. What are the facts, data, or logic that will help influence your stakeholders?

2. Whom do you need to consult with before you try to influence your stakeholders?

3. If someone helps you, how might you help them? What's the give and take?

4. Whom can you enlist to help you influence your stakeholders?

5. Are there any pressure tactics that might get your stakeholders moving?

6. Who could endorse you and legitimize what you are trying to influence?

7. Sometimes influence requires assertiveness. Have you considered saying to your stakeholders, "My vision is X. What will it take to get you on board?"

8. How might you get access to the most senior movers and shakers?

9. How can you show your stakeholders you have truly listened to their needs and considered their point of view?

10. What will appeal to your stakeholders' hearts and/or values?

11. What will unify your stakeholders so that they all see the value in what you are trying to influence?

12. There is a saying: "Others won't hear you unless they feel supported by you." How might this be true here?

13. If you scratch your stakeholders' backs, will they scratch yours?

14. Where do you need to be patient?

15. How can you best establish your credibility?

16. When you consider your stakeholders, what interests do you share with them?

17. What's a win-win way forward?

4. Considering Politics and Power

1. Who has power in this organization?

2. Would you say you have the power to influence change? Why, or why not?

3. What information or expertise would give you more power?

4. What relationships would give you some power?

5. What do you have or know that others consider valuable?

6. What politics do you need to be aware of?

7. What mixed messages are you getting from your stakeholders?

8. Who tends to say one thing but does something else altogether?

9. Is there anyone who might try to sabotage your efforts?

10. Do people tend to view you as a political player? How do you know?

11. If you win and get what you want, who might lose?

5. Communicating Your Message and Persuading Others to Act

1. What's the key point you want to make?

2. What's the elevator pitch that will help you sell your idea?

3. How can you frame your idea so that people are primed to listen to what you have to say?

4. What message will appeal to people's hearts?

5. What can you communicate to inspire others to act?

6. What evidence or data can you use to back up your claim?

7. How can you make your message so simple a five-year-old would understand it?

8. What's a meaningful story that highlights your key message?

9. What separates ordinary communication from persuasive communication?

10. What distinguishes ethical persuasion from manipulation?

11. What information will change your stakeholders' minds?

12. What is your body language saying?

13. As you communicate about your influence goals, what values do you want to hold front and center?

14. What's a question you get asked all the time? How can you polish up your answer?

15. What's the key takeaway message you want people to understand?

16. What type of message would resonate with your audience?

17. What are you doing and/or saying that is contradictory to your key message?

18. What are three things you can do to reinforce your message?

19. What are the biggest communication mistakes you tend to make?

20. When you think about your stakeholders, how is their communication style similar/different from yours? What implications does this have for your communication tactics?

BUTTERFLY

We all have hardened parts of ourselves, little spaces inside we carefully protect. A safe exchange built on trust enables us to venture into these parts of ourselves.

2.5 Delegating

Delegation is crucial for a leader's success. It enables leaders to elevate their contribution and empower others. Effective delegation starts with being clear about what you want to delegate, whom you will delegate to, and how you will set them up to succeed. There are many obstacles to effective delegation, including being unwilling to let go and share power. Sometimes leaders don't delegate because they want to protect their team members from getting "too busy" or because they fear others cannot do the work as well as they can.

1. Identifying What to Delegate

1. What would free you up to do more strategic work?

2. In your role, where do you add the most value? What do you need to let go of to focus on high-value activities?

3. In your role, what are your top twenty activities? Which of these activities are strategic? Which are personally energizing? Which are time wasters?

4. In your role, where do you need and/or want to be hands-on?

5. What are you currently doing that would be a great learning opportunity for someone else?

6. Is there anything to which you have said "yes" to that you should have said "no" to?

7. What can you take off your plate?

8. How much of your time is focused on tomorrow instead of today?

2. Identifying Whom to Delegate To

1. Whom do you need to develop to elevate your own contribution?

2. Who are the stars on your team?

3. Consider each team member: Would you rehire them today? Why, or why not?

4. Who wants to do this work even more than you do?

5. Whom do you totally trust to do this work well?

6. Who needs to learn how to do this work?

7. Whom are you concerned about delegating to?

3. Delegating a Task or Project

1. What is this person's skill level to do this job? High, medium, or low?

2. What is their motivation? High, medium, or low?

3. Have you given them a clear goal for the assignment?

4. What part of this task/project do they need to do well?

5. Where will the person be stretched?

6. What support and/or training do they need to be effective?

7. After delegating, what checks and balances would be helpful?

8. What if they fail? What implications will this have for the business?

9. How can you empower this person to succeed?

10. What distinguishes delegating work from dumping work on others?

4. Overcoming Obstacles to Delegation

1. Why don't you delegate as much as you should or could?

2. What are the signals that you need to delegate more?

3. Why are you spending so much time on tactical issues?

4. What beliefs hold you back from delegating?

5. One obstacle to delegation may be that you enjoy doing some aspects of your work and don't want to delegate them. Would you say this is true for you?

6. One obstacle to delegation is a fear that team members can't do the work as quickly or as well as you can. Would you say this is true for you? If you continue to hold this belief, where might it lead you?

7. Another obstacle to delegating is the worry that you will overload team members. How are you trying to protect your people? Yourself?

8. A desire for control and/or other perfectionist tendencies can be obstacles to delegation. Where might your standards be too high? What would help you let those go?

9. In what situations do you tend to micromanage?

10. What does your approach to delegation say about your level of trust in others?

DUCK

Most of us talk too much.
It's an ongoing act of self-discipline to
be quiet.

2.6 Working through Conflict

A conflict often begins with a misunderstanding that esca-
lates into judgments, assumptions, and fears. One of the
hardest parts of being in a conflict is experiencing escalat-
ing emotions and the fight-or-flight response. In a healthy
relationship, conflict is a sign that two people are investing
in each other. In an unhealthy relationship, it is a sign that
they might abandon each other. Resolving conflicts requires
maturity and communication.

1. Becoming Aware of a Conflict

1. What's this conflict about?

2. What evidence is there that a conflict exists?

3. What are your hopes and fears in this situation?

4. If you resolve this conflict, what might the best
    possible outcome be?

5. If you resolve this conflict, what might the worst possible outcome be?

6. If this conflict goes unresolved, what will the impact be?

7. What behaviors or beliefs will lead to the best possible outcome?

8. What part are you playing in this conflict?

9. To understand the situation better, what information or facts that you're missing now do you need to have?

10. How does this conflict fit into a bigger context for you? For the opposing party?

2. Dealing with Emotions in Conflict Situations

1. What feelings are coming up for you?

2. What do your feelings remind you of? Anything from the past?

3. If you let these feelings get the better of you, where might that lead you?

4. What is triggering a defensive reaction in you? In others?

5. **Fight, flight, or freeze? Which one tends to come up for you?**

6. Are there any feelings that seem intense or exaggerated, given the circumstances?

7. What's it like to be in the hot seat right now?

8. Beyond this disagreement, what binds you to the person you are experiencing conflict with?

3. Listening and Showing You Care about the Person Whom You Are in Conflict With

1. There is a wonderful saying that we are all responsible for 50 percent of the relationship dynamics we find ourselves in. What's your 50 percent responsibility for this conflict?

2. Put yourself in the other person's shoes. What might they want or need?

3. What can you say, do, or not do to show you understand this person?

4. What are the barriers that prevent you from really listening to each other?

5. What if you decide to pull together instead of push against each other? What would that look and feel like?

6. Where do you see eye to eye with this person? What's the common ground?

7. Anything you want to apologize for?

8. How forthright have you been about communicating what is important to you?

4. Using Conflict as an Opportunity for Growth

1. Conflict can be viewed as an opportunity for personal awakening. When you consider this conflict, what opportunity for awakening might exist for you?

2. Why did this conflict come to you at this time? What's the purpose in it for your own life path?

3. What annoys you about the other person? How might this be a mirror for your own shadow (that part of you that you don't like or keep hidden from view)?

4. What are your values? If you were being true to your values, how would you attempt to resolve this conflict?

5. When you imagine living your values when resolving this conflict, what worries or fears are coming up for you?

6. If you saw a video of yourself in this conflict, would you look or sound like one of your parents?

7. What's the difference between moving through this conflict and getting caught up in it?

8. Tell me about how the different parts of you want to respond. The wise, calm part? The defensive part? Other parts of you?

9. What are you doing or not doing that prevents you from resolving this conflict?

10. What's stopping you from responding calmly?

11. What are the imaginary arguments you're having in your head with this person?

5. Resolving Conflicts

1. When you imagine resolving this conflict, what would be the highest and best outcome?

2. How do you hope this conflict will be resolved?

3. What is a win-win outcome?

4. What's the high road?

5. What strengths do you have that could support the resolution of this conflict?

6. What would help you feel safe when addressing this conflict?

7. How do you propose you move forward?

8. If you resolve this in a positive way, what's the payoff?

9. If you stay in this conflict, what's the payoff?

10. What are the skills or support you need to navigate through this?

11. What's the bigger future you want to create together?

12. What's just beyond the conflict?

13. If your next meeting with this person were filmed and got more than one million hits on YouTube, what would you hope to observe?

14. What are the signs it is time to walk away?

 BUTTERFLY

Encourage: To inspire with courage, spirit, or hope (Merriam-Webster.com, February 2017).

Section 3

LEADING THE ORGANIZATION

> Strategy is about making choices,
> trade-offs, it's about deliberately
> choosing to be different.
> —*Michael Porter*

Ever go into a strategic planning session wishing you had some fresh questions to ask? Questions that will blow open the team's thinking and expand the possibilities being considered for the future of the business? Your wish is granted! This section includes a collection of questions that will help you fine-tune your organizational strategy, step up innovation, improve your culture, and more.

Personally, I use these questions with executive teams, either as openers to set the tone for a strategic day or to help a team explore important topics, such as competitive differentiation or operational excellence. Doing this sharpens the conversation, helps the team make sense of complicated topics, and orients the team around relevant points. My hope is that you will find some gems here too—questions that unlock the strategic potential in your organization and your top teams.

3. Leading Organizations

DUCK

A good listener has a contemplative
attitude and an open mind.

BUTTERFLY

When you notice a question boosts the
energy in the room, you have struck gold.

3.1 Setting a Vision and Strategy

Strategy is like a North Star, illuminating the path ahead. It helps to define common purpose, clarifies differentiation, and considers the industry and market conditions. The best strategies lead to growth and clear priorities.

1. Clarifying the Organization's Purpose

1. Why does this organization exist?

2. Whom does the organization ultimately serve?

3. What is the value this organization provides to the community?

4. How does this organization make a difference in people's lives?

5. What do we, as an organization, genuinely care about?

6. What are our goals and aspirations?

7. What inspires us to go the extra mile?

8. What central purpose runs across all our stakeholders—customers, partners, employees, and suppliers?

9. What is the thing we are uniquely capable of—the thing that only this organization can do?

10. What are our core values?

11. What are our primary objectives?

12. In your view, what constitutes a more inspiring future for this business?

13. If this company shuts down tomorrow, what impact would that have on the community?

2. Sharpening Competitive Differentiation

1. What do our customers value about us?

2. What makes us unique?

3. Where do we want to play?

4. What do we believe differentiates us from our competitors?

5. Do our customers value our key differentiators? Are the differentiators truly unique to us?

6. What evidence is there to support our differentiators?

7. How can we embed our differentiation across the customer value chain?

8. If a competitor were going to put us out of business, how would they do it?

9. What is something we can offer our customers that they would find it impossible to say "no" to?

10. Imagine we charged twice as much for our services as our competitors do. What would be the value proposition we would use to justify this?

11. How will we win in the marketplace?

12. If we do good work, what benefits will our customers experience?

13. What are the major rules and sacred cows in our industry? What if we tear up the rule book?

14. What does it mean for us to put our money where our heart is?

15. What would we be proud to sell and recommend to our family and friends?

16. Let's come up with ten ways we could really mess up our competitive differentiation. Where are we exhibiting these tendencies now, and how can we eliminate them?

17. What are the ways we want to continue to set the bar in our industry?

3. Spotting Opportunities for Growth

1. Where is our biggest growth potential?

2. What would it take to double our business every eighteen months?

3. What do you think it would take for the company to double in size in two years?

4. If you have ever worked for a fast-growing start-up, you know you can pack twenty years of experience and growth into two years. What might leapfrog our growth now?

5. Where do we want to be in five years, and why?

6. Where is demand increasing? Declining?

7. What opportunities do we have to make money 24-7?

8. What's the value we see sitting in our sales pipeline?

9. Where do we want to make a quantum leap?

10. What's some uncharted territory we want to explore?

11. What are our barriers to growth?

12. How much capital do we need to grow the business?

13. Is there a way to grow with very little investment?

14. Is there something we can invest in today that will generate cash for years to come?

15. Do we believe we have the potential to be number one?

16. Why can't we be the best in our field? Why not us?

4. Establishing Goals and Clarifying Focus

1. What do we want our big moment to be this year?

2. What are the wins that will change everything for us?

3. What will build momentum?

4. What are our goals and priorities?

5. Do we have the right mix of quick wins and "shoot for the moon" initiatives?

6. Could we argue that if our goals don't require some element of luck and "right place, right time," then we are thinking too small?

7. Let's challenge the idea that "once-in-a-lifetime opportunities" are rare. What's the once-in-a-lifetime opportunity we have today?

8. What reality do we need to face?

9. What risks would be fun to take?

10. What good ideas did we have last year that didn't bear fruit? Any goals we want to resurrect?

11. If we look at our success and/or stability as temporary, what becomes a priority?

12. What metrics are most important for benchmarking our success?

13. What's our scorecard?

DUCK

Consider whether you are listening to all the
voices that need to be heard.

3.2 Driving Innovation

Innovation is about anticipating and meeting future needs, spotting breakthrough opportunities, and uncovering continuous improvement opportunities, such as finding ways to deliver a product or service with less effort. When company practices enable innovation, the tactic becomes embedded in a company's culture.

1. Thinking about the Future

1. If you could bet on a key idea for the future, what would you bet on?

2. Tell me something that you think is important for this company's future and that you worry the executive team is ignoring.

3. What's a dumb idea that might be smart for the future of our business?

4. The world is marked by exponential change. What might this mean for our products and services in the future?

5. What do you think would be cool to experience in your lifetime?

6. In your view, what are the world's grand challenges?

7. Some say the next generation will do more in a day than previous generations did in a lifetime. What might this mean for this company's future?

8. What do we accept as "the way things are" that may no longer be true in the future?

9. What are we putting off doing today that will benefit our company twenty years from now?

10. What technologies will likely disrupt this industry?

2. Spotting Opportunities to Innovate in the Company

1. If you took two weeks to do nothing but think, what would you want to think about?

2. What's the easiest and fastest way for us to make more money?

3. How can we help our customers get more of what they want?

4. In your view, what should we be spending extravagantly on, and why?

5. What do we notice our competitors investing in? Assuming they are pretty smart, why might they be making these choices?

6. What's the number one reason we don't always win?

7. When we look around the company, where would we benefit from thinking like a start-up again?

8. If we had to sell our product for $5, how would we make money doing that?

9. If we were to set up a company to compete with ours, how would we do it?

10. What is threatening this business?

3. Viewing Innovation as Continuous Improvement

1. Consider our core product or service. If we only had 10 percent of our current budget, how would we change the way we deliver this service or make this product?

2. Simplicity is the ultimate sophistication. How can we make our company practices simpler?

3. What if one hour per day of our best work was all we needed to accelerate our innovation? What would we do in that one hour?

4. If a new hotshot innovation expert took over our company today, what do you think they would look at and say, "You are in the dark ages."

5. What if we could get from point A to point B in half the time? What would it take?

6. Imagine we could systematically focus on three high-impact priorities per year instead of one

hundred different things. What would we focus on, and why?

7. Although it is common to want to avoid crises and emergencies, these are often major catalysts for innovation and growth. What can we learn from our darker days?

8. What are some new applications for our core skills?

9. What is your 20 percent solution (your idea for improving service, quality, or results by 20 percent)?

10. Pick a key business process. Can we get this process down to two steps?

11. What would elevate our customer experience?

12. What would improve our key result areas by 1,000 percent?

4. Company Practices That Enable Innovation

1. What does innovation mean to our company?

2. Which function or role has the responsibility to drive innovation?

3. How do we spot and nurture innovation in the company?

4. What approach will help our employees to innovate?

5. Around the world, what companies are driving global innovation? What are they doing that we are not?

6. What metrics used in our organization measure the value of innovation practices?

7. Do you believe our team is diverse enough to generate innovative ideas?

8. When you are doing what's never been done before, there is no map or instruction book. Given this, what are the values, beliefs, or principles that will help us innovate?

9. How might we work with our competitors to innovate within our industry?

3.3 Enhancing the Customer Experience

Having a customer-centered culture and excellent customer experience often leads to competitive differentiation. Optimizing the customer experience involves mapping the customer journey from start to finish and finding opportunities to add value to customers each step of the way.

1. Understanding the Customer Landscape and How It Impacts a Business

1. Describe what being a customer-obsessed business means to you.

2. When was the last time you had an amazing customer experience?

3. In your experience, what company goes out of its way to provide the best customer experience possible?

4. How is the digital world shaping the future of selling to our customers?

5. Some say that in the modern world, what you do is less important than how you do it. How might this be relevant to our customers?

6. Who is our ideal current customer? Our ideal prospective customer?

7. How are our customers' expectations changing?

8. How might we use artificial intelligence to understand our customers' habits better and serve them accordingly?

2. Optimizing the Customer Experience

1. When our customers interact with us, what do they hope to experience?

2. What are all the key touch points for our customer experience?

3. How differentiated is our customer experience in the marketplace?

4. At each touchpoint, what are the customer-facing activities? What are the internal activities?

5. What are our customers' feelings, motivations, and questions at each touchpoint?

6. What are our customers' pain points?

7. What do we want the start and the end of the customer experience to look like?

8. Let's look at our products and services through the lens of our customers' emotions: ease, empowerment, frustration, and so forth. What opportunities do we see?

9. What information do our customers expect to have instant access to?

10. Where are our biggest opportunities for personalization?

11. What are the hidden treasures in our customer feedback?

12. What do our customers want that we are currently not delivering?

13. In what ways are we becoming irrelevant to customers?

14. What would blow our customers' minds?

BUTTERFLY
Be careful of "why" questions. They can feel like judgments when open curiosity is absent.

3.4 Leading Change

Leading change within an organization begins with spotting an opportunity to make things better and having a vision for the future. Aligning key stakeholders around the vision and considering how a change initiative impacts others increases the odds of success. A robust communication plan and change campaign can inspire people to get on board with a change effort and help overcome their resistance. Technology is strategically used to enable instant ongoing communication.

1. Helping a Team Create the Case for Change in an Organization

1. What is the purpose of this change?

2. If we make this change, what will be different in the future?

3. With this change, what does success look, feel, and sound like?

4. Why are we making this change?

5. How is this change aligned with our top goals/ business strategy?

6. With this change, what value will we create for the organization?

7. What problem are we trying to solve?

8. How will this change improve our work?

9. How will this change improve our capabilities?

10. What opportunity are we going after?

11. What's inspiring about this change?

12. How does this change fit with our values?

13. What's the business case?

14. What are the costs? The benefits?

15. What outcome would exceed our wildest dreams?

16. What obstacles need to be overcome?

17. What's the risk of not changing?

2. Defining the Best Approach for a Change Effort in an Organization

1. What's different about leading change in the digital age?

2. What leadership behaviors and management systems are required to support this change?

3. What's the personal touch that will help this change stick?

4. What will be the cross-functional impacts of this change?

5. What is the shift in thinking or mindset needed for this change?

6. Lots of change efforts fail. What's one thing we must get right?

7. What's an inclusive way to lead this change?

8. What will have people enthusiastically support this?

9. What are the politics we need to watch out for?

10. What are the key milestones?

11. What are some quick wins that will lead to positive momentum?

12. Would you say we need to slow down our efforts or speed them up?

13. What if we just let things unfold?

14. As the organization goes through this change, what do we want to stay the same?

15. What's different about this change effort compared to other change efforts? What's the same?

16. What good advice about change management are we completely ignoring?

17. What could go wrong?

18. Where might we lose motivation to see this through?

19. What training do people need?

3. Aligning Stakeholders around a Vision for Change

1. Who is the executive sponsor? What is their role? Do we believe they understand and are committed to this role?

2. Who is the project manager (PM)? What are the more complicated issues the PM will likely have to deal with?

3. What kind of issues are important to escalate to the sponsor?

4. Who are our most important change champions?

5. Who are the early adopters? The detractors?

6. What impact will this change have on staff? Customers?

7. What's different about this team's needs versus that team's? What's the same?

8. Who will be happy about this?

9. Who might be hurt by this?

10. What are the stakeholders' competing demands?

11. What is the commitment level we anticipate?

12. Who needs to be on board?

4. Crafting a Message about Why the Change Matters

1. Why are we making this change? What's the core of our message?

2. What's a compelling story that highlights why this change matters?

3. What, specifically, will be different if this change goes well?

4. What data or research brings credibility to our approach?

5. Why does this change matter to you, the leader, on a personal level?

6. If this change goes well, what is in it for others?

7. What's a story that will build excitement about this change?

8. What objections or questions do we anticipate? How will we respond?

5. Creating a Communication Campaign to Support the Change Effort

1. What's an energizing way to kick this off?

2. Who can speak passionately about this?

3. What's an engaging way to communicate about this?

4. How can we simplify the communication process?

5. Where might communication break down?

6. Who won't be that great at communicating this message?

7. How can we help people communicate more effectively?

8. What technologies can help us to communicate with our stakeholders?

9. What can we change in our physical environment to reinforce our key message?

10. What takeaway would your stakeholders find useful?

11. What informal networks can we leverage to communicate about this change?

12. How will we respond to cynicism about this change effort?

BUTTERFLY

 A question can reveal a blind spot—an opportunity for growth that may not be apparently obvious.

3.5 Managing Operations

Optimizing systems to support growth and finding opportunities to create efficiencies strengthen a company over the long term. Equally important are managing money, optimizing cash, and strategically allocating resources toward the top priorities.

1. Optimizing Systems to Support Growth

1. What will it take to scale and grow the business?

2. What are the key scaling challenges?

3. What's the bold action that will lead to growth?

4. What are the systems that support our team's big ideas?

5. What are the core activities that we need to focus on to support growth?

6. What do we want to start doing, stop doing, and keep doing in order to scale the business?

7. To free up strategic capacity, what's our biggest opportunity for automation?

8. Have we built our systems for today or tomorrow?

2. Finding Opportunities to Create Efficiencies

1. How can we ensure that each step in our business processes generates value?

2. Complete this sentence: In the future, this process would be better if we _____.

3. Name the feeling you have about this process or system. Consider words such as irritating, easy, frustrating, and painless.

4. What's going well with our systems that we don't want to change?

5. How can we make our systems more environmentally friendly?

6. How can we make our systems predictable and scalable?

7. How can we make our systems more flexible?

8. Where would we benefit from automation?

9. What if the person responsible for this process went on vacation for six months? Would it still work?

10. Can a robot do this work?

11. How can we streamline our production/sales cycle?

12. Is it possible to do this process in a minute or less?

13. What are we micromanaging? What is this behavior telling us about our systems?

14. Where is complexity increasing our chance of failure?

15. Where do we need better information flow?

16. Where is accountability lax?

17. What's our strategy for optimizing capacity?

18. What internal controls will help keep us on track?

19. Where might we want to give up some control?

20. What will motivate people to be more efficient?

3. Managing Money and Optimizing Cash

1. What will help us better forecast our revenue and operating costs?

2. Where is our capital being tied up? What can we do to free up cash?

3. What disciplines are most important for managing cash?

4. What are our highest margin activities?

5. Does everyone understand how we make money?

6. To what extent have we aligned our financial resources with our critical priorities?

7. How can we improve financial terms in our customer contracts to optimize cash?

8. What actions can we take to have more visible and reliable financial reporting?

9. What is our process for managing and approving capital spending?

10. If we were able to free up cash, what would we do with it?

11. What financial controls would give us comfort?

12. Where are we burning cash? Why?

DUCK

Effective listeners are able to reflect back what they have heard, holding up a mirror for others.

3.6 Energizing Culture

Culture reminds me of the space between my thoughts during a meditation. It's hard to put my finger on it, yet I know it is profoundly important. In order to create a culture that is a source of competitive differentiation, it is critical to explore the current culture, the ideal culture, and the gap between the two, so that an action plan can be created. Ideally, the action plan is built around a set of core principles, and there are carefully crafted cultural practices that send a message about what is valued and what is not tolerated.

1. Exploring the Current Culture with a Team or Employee

1. What do you love about working here?

2. What makes our culture different?

3. What stories are iconic in our culture?

4. Would you say our culture supports self-actualization? Why, or why not?

5. What's the thread of gold in our culture?

6. What's the link between our culture and our profitability?

7. What truth do we need to face about our culture?

8. What cultural imperfections do we want to celebrate?

9. In our culture, how do we tend to overuse our strengths? What are the implications of this?

10. What's the dark side of our culture?

11. What are the contradictions that are alive and well in our culture?

12. What's the gap between what we say and what we tend to do?

13. What's the gap between how we feel and what we tend to say?

14. What's the gap between what we say in a performance review and what we later say about the people we've reviewed?

15. To what extent do our values shape our current culture?

16. In what ways is our culture a reflection of our leaders?

17. What are the cultural practices that really matter to us?

18. Who are the five most respected people in the organization? What cultural traits do they share?

19. What are the common traits among those employees who have failed to thrive in our culture?

20. Who tends to get privileges around here, and who doesn't?

21. What feels high risk around here?

2. Defining the Desired Culture

1. What does a winning culture look like to us?

2. What do we want employees to say about working here?

3. Think about the best workplace culture you have ever been a part of. What made it great?

4. What's the unique story behind this company? How is this story kept alive in the culture?

5. What is the primary message we want employees to get about our culture?

6. What are the stories or artifacts that bring these cultural messages to life?

7. Can you describe our ideal company culture in three to five words?

8. What are the values and/or principles we want to build our culture around?

9. What is our cultural promise?

10. What is our employee value proposition?

11. What are eight distinguishing characteristics of our desired culture?

12. If our desired culture were a movie, what movie would it be?

13. What are the beliefs that will help us succeed and create the desired culture?

3. Changing Culture in a Company

1. If we could rewrite our culture, what would we change?

2. Draw a picture of our current culture, our desired culture, and what you think it will take to make this shift to the latter.

3. What would create more unity between our internal culture and our external brand?

4. What can we do every day to nurture our desired culture?

5. What business practices need to align with our culture?

6. What pressures make it difficult for us to take action toward our desired culture?

7. How can we transform our onboarding process into a cultural experience?

8. What will help people flourish?

9. How does our culture impact the quality of our decisions?

10. What changes to our physical space would convey what this culture is becoming?

11. What are some ways we can align our rewards with our desired culture?

12. When we tried to change our culture in the past, what worked? What didn't?

13. What data do we pay attention to when measuring cultural health?

Bonus Section

MAKING THE WORLD A BETTER PLACE

Each one of us has an opportunity to make a positive difference in the world—to bring hope to future generations. These questions will help you and your teams broaden your impact, and think deeply about what matters.

1. What are the problems in the world that are most likely to impact the future of humanity?

2. What do you hope is possible for our nation? All nations?

3. What do you hope is possible for the human race?

4. If you could put 5 percent of your time toward something deeply meaningful to you or the world, what would you do?

5. If you could write a message that would get through to all of humanity, what would your message be?

6. What would you like to be different in the world for the next generation?

7. What's the transformation you want to see in the world?

8. What kind of world do you want to live in?

9. How is technology changing what it feels like to be human?

10. In the future, what role might technology play in shaping morals and ethics?

11. What would make the world a better place?

12. In your view, what would be a huge step forward for humankind?

13. How can we use our entrepreneurial skills to tackle social or global problems?

14. What is the peace you need to discover within yourself that will enable you to bring about positive change in the world?

15. Why is now the greatest time to be alive?

16. Do you really need all your stuff?

17. As a planet and a global community, we are at a crossroads of collective evolution and total collapse. What scenarios will lead us to a brighter future?

18. What is a more conscious way of engaging with the planet?

19. What is a cruelty-free alternative to meat production we can consider?

20. What changes in the world when we treasure all sentient beings?

21. Many people believe that the state of the world is a reflection of human consciousness. What do you believe?

22. In your view, how much energy has humanity invested in cultivating inner peace and happiness? What are the implications of this?

23. What is the most constructive use of your creativity?

24. What's the next step beyond recycling?

25. What does being a good citizen mean to you?

26. What if you are the "somebody" who should do something about the state of the world?

27. What is the future you want your children to inherit?

28. What is the most important conversation for our time?

29. What's the worldwide cultural shift that will heal the planet?

30. What's the climate change conversation you want to have?

31. How can we make better use of what we have?

32. How can you decrease your energy consumption by 75 percent?

33. What's freeing about minimalism?

34. In your view, how is the world getting better?

35. Whom can you collaborate with to broaden your impact?

36. What's your carbon footprint?

37. Who is responsible for carbon emissions?

38. What's the precedent you want to set?

39. What are you wasting?

40. Every person has an opportunity to co-create our world. What do you want your contribution to be?

41. What is holding you back from making positive changes?

42. What are some specific actions you can take in order to make positive changes now?

43. What's a no-brainer for making a difference?

BUTTERFLY

Don't be afraid to probe. The best ideas are often three layers down.

Final Thoughts:

A NEW VANTAGE POINT

As you continue to experiment with these questions, consider this: the best questions for personal growth are not
necessarily the ones you or others are initially attracted to.
Push yourself to ask questions that go beyond your comfort
zone. Don't fall into the trap of asking only the questions
that confirm your prevailing viewpoint. By stretching your
comfort zone, you will start to see issues from a fresh perspective and expand your team's vantage point.

Personally, I find that provocative questions often seem a bit
off-putting at first, yet in the end they offer an opportunity
for growth. They tap into people's hearts or intuition, they
open up a new perspective, and/or they reveal a relationship between elements that people may not have previously
considered. I know I have hit the jackpot when a question
prompts a pause. It must sink in before it can be answered

adequately. This experience feels different compared to asking a comfortable question—one that fits within the boundaries of what people already know and prefer.

Asking uncomfortable questions won't always be easy, because of the confirmation bias and the inner judge. The confirmation bias is the tendency to seek out information that confirms preexisting beliefs. It steers us to the familiar. Similarly, the inner judge (that pesky inner voice that has an opinion about everything) will work hard to maintain the status quo. Your inner judge will likely evaluate each question, saying things such as, "Oh, this question is too off the wall." "That question is too weird." "People will think I am nuts if I ask that question."

I encourage you to notice the inner judge and confirmation bias, put them aside, and go bravely ahead. Experiment with a wide variety of questions, including the ones that give you pause or even turn you off at first. When asking unconventional questions, consider framing them with a phrase such as, "This question may seem out of left field, but let's see what we can learn from it." This will let people know you are about to move out of familiar and comfortable territory.

This leads to one final question for you to consider. (It seems only fitting that we finish this book with a question, doesn't it?) As you come back to this book again and again, ask yourself:

What are the questions that will take you out of your element and personal comfort zone, and hurl you into the mysterious unknown?

ABOUT THE AUTHOR

Natalie is one of those people who always needs a little project on the go to stay inspired. This coaching book was her passion project for two years. She would listen to podcasts, read white papers, cruise the web, and turn fascinating talks into questions.

She created this book because she noticed a pattern: her clients wanted to be better coaches, but they struggled to come up with good coaching questions. Being a practical type, she wanted to fill this need.

Natalie is an executive coach. Her specialty is working with CEOs and executives who want to make significant contributions to their organizations and society. After more than a decade doing this work, she still loves it.

You can learn more about Natalie at
www.waterfront-partners.com

Key References

I formed most of the questions in this book by drawing on my fifteen years of experience as a coach and consultant and by translating concepts in articles, books, and videos into questions. However, there were some resources that inspired me again and again, so I have listed them here. If nothing else, the references make a terrific reading list.

SECTION 1

Richard Barrett, *A New Psychology of Human Well-Being: An Exploration of the Influence of Ego-Soul Dynamics on Mental and Physical Health* (Richard Barrett Fulfilling Books, 2016).

Aaron T. Beck and Christine A. Padesky, *Mind over Mood*, Kindle Edition (Guilford, 2015).

Nathaniel Branden, *How to Raise Your Self-Esteem: The Proven Action-Oriented Approach to Greater Self-Respect and Self-Confidence*, Kindle Edition (Bantam, 2011).

Julia Cameron, *It's Never Too Late to Begin Again: Discovering Creativity and Meaning at Midlife and Beyond*, Kindle Edition (Tarcher Perigree, 2016).

Robert Kegan and Lisa Laskow Lahey, *Immunity to Change: How to Overcome It and Unlock the Potential in Yourself and Your Organization (Leadership for the Common Good)*, Kindle Edition (Harvard Business Review Press, 2009).

Mark Nepo, *The Endless Practice: Becoming Who You Were Born to Be*, Kindle Edition (Atria Books, 2014).

Websites
Ramit Sethi: *http://www.iwillteachyoutoberich.com/*

SECTION 2

Timothy Ferriss and Arnold Schwarzenegger, *Tools of Titans: The Tactics, Routines, and Habits of Billionaires, Icons, and World-Class Performers* (Houghton Mifflin, 2016).

Colin Gautrey, *Advocates and Enemies: How to Build Practical Strategies to Influence Your Stakeholders* (Gautrey Group, 2011).

Otto E. Laske, *Measuring Hidden Dimensions of Human Systems* (Laske and Associates, 2009).

Richard McGuigan, *Shadows, Conflict, and the Mediator*, Conflict Resolution Quarterly 26, no. 3 (2009).

SECTION 3

Chip Heath and Dan Heath, *Made to Stick* (Random House, 2007).

Robert Kegan and Lisa Laskow Lahey, *An Everyone Culture: Becoming a Deliberately Developmental Organization*, Kindle Edition (Harvard Business Review Press, 2016).

W. Chan Kim and Renée Mauborgne, *Blue Ocean Strategy, Expanded Edition: How to Create Uncontested Market Space and Make the Competition Irrelevant*, Kindle Edition (Harvard Business Review Press, 2014).

Robin Gregory McLaughlin, *Shadow Work in Support of the Adult Developmental Journey*, unpublished PhD diss., Lesley University, 2014.

Alexander Osterwalder and Yves Pigneur, *Value Proposition Design: How to Create Products and Services Customers Want*, Kindle Edition (Wiley, 2014).

Websites
Fortune: *http://fortune.com/tag/10-questions/*

Harvard Business Review: *https://hbr.org/2010/05/the-five-questions-of-strategy*

Lean Labs: *https://www.lean-labs.com/blog/creating-a-brand-identity-20-questions-to-consider*

Singularity University: *https://su.org/*

Made in the USA
Columbia, SC
10 July 2020